SEASONAL HERBS
from Caprilands
Step-by-Step in the Garden

Adelma Grenier Simmons

Photographs by
George Gregory Wieser

**MALLARD
PRESS**

Copyright © 1991 by Adelma Grenier Simmons
Photographs copyright © 1991 by George Gregory Wieser

Mallard Press and its accompanying design and logo are trademarks of
BDD Promotional Book Company, Inc.
First published in the United States of America in 1991 by Mallard Press,
an imprint of BDD Promotional Book Company, Inc.
666 Fifth Avenue
New York, NY 10103
ISBN 0-7924-5620-3

Editorial Development by Beverly Pennacchini
Design, Typography and Production by Tony Meisel
Styling by Laurie Pepin
Origination and Printing by
Impresora Donneco International, S.A. de C.V.

Produced by Wieser & Wieser, Inc.
118 East 25th Street, New York, NY 10010

Printed in MEXICO.

CONTENTS

Introduction

HERBS ARE FOREVER

The friend of the physician and the pride of cooks.
Virgil

Happy is the herb gardener through all the seasons and the years. Spring, summer, autumn and winter-all have added meaning, for to each season the garden yields a special taste and presents a picture uniquely its own.

The exploration of herbs dates back five thousand years before Christ. Down through the ages the great and the small have shared a fascination with herbs. Charlatans and scholars, peasants and priests, physicians and magicians have contributed their observations upon which herbs heal, which taste good, and which scare away evil spirits from haunting the safety of our autumn hearth.

Caprilands Herb Farm in Coventry, Connecticut continues the tradition of herbal study and enjoyment. What was in 1929, a barren plot surrounded with the wreckage of years of mismanagement,is today fifty garden acres dedicated exclusively to the cultivation, preservation and appreciation of herbs.

In reality, you can derive hours of study and pleasure without moving far from a sunny windowsill or a cozy seat by the fire. You may plant an herb garden that knows no size, but may be as large or small as your imagination reaches.

Plan and sow your seeds, enjoy your harvests, make herbal vinegars and sweet pomanders, trace herbal uses from their earliest origins in song and story until their enchantment lays a gentle hold on your daily life.

The herbs at Caprilands in full bloom.

6

SPRING

Spring Diary

In Spring my hands are aching for the touch of warm soil, and my eyes ready for the greens and yellows of the new season after winter's browns and grays. My mind is filled with things to do. I've pots of well-started plants to go out, and seed packets a-plenty to be sown directly in the garden. I have stacks of diagrams outlining where to put what and why. My soil amendments wait, ready for the wheelbarrow. Spring is a season hectic with growth and activity, and as I walk back to the house, I know that very soon, there will be no time to dream over a cup of tea.

Soil Preparation and Planting

Soil Preparation

The "perfect" site for an herb garden is well-drained, with a slight slope so that water does not linger round the crowns of plants. A neutral to slightly alkaline or sweet soil is best for most herbs. Herbs profit by eight hours of sunshine daily. Of course, no site is ever perfect, and the challenge is to select the right herb for the right location and favorites will grow to some extent, even under trying conditions.

After you select your site, stake out boundaries and remove any large debris. Work the soil to a depth of 12 inches using a tiller or spade. I recommend three rototillings or diggings: the first to remove sticks and stones, the second to incorporate well-rotted compost or cow manure, and a third to mix in garden lime if your soil is too acidic (under 7.0 pH).

7

Planting

I find that all herb seeds do better if they are started outdoors where fresh air, full light and coolness promote vigorous growth. When frost danger is past and you have prepared your soil, mark out rows, clumps or groupings with a hoe, making them wide enough to do a little scattering. Sprinkle the seeds over the prepared area, scatter soil lightly over them, then moisten with a mist spray of water from the hose. The general rule is to cover seeds to a depth that is three times their thickness. Keep the seeded area moist until germination is well along, and be patient, herbs are slow to germinate.

If you have to have plants early, start them in February or March in the sunniest and coolest window you have, or under fluorescent lights. Annuals to try early include basil, summery savory, sweet marjoram, dill parsley, chervil and calendula.

Plant in flats or boxes filled with a mixture of two parts sand and one part vermiculite. Moisten well, then sow the seeds and barely cover them. Keep in a well-lighted place and water from the bottom as often as necessary. As soon as germination starts, move containers into the sun. When seedlings are large enough to handle, transplant them to pots filled with a mixture of equal parts vermiculite, garden loam and compost. The seedlings need a nighttime temperature of 50 to 60 degrees and plenty of fresh air in the daytime.

As spring approaches, harden off the seedlings by sinking the small pots down in the soil of a coldframe. Or you can group the seed flats on a protected porch for a few days. After this hardening off, the seedlings will be ready for planting directly in the garden.

It is a good idea to give some thought to companion planting. The philosophy behind companion planting is that many common garden pests find being in the vicinity of certain common plants repugnant, and certain common plants grow better near other plants. Consult the glossary of herbs for companion planting suggestions.

Top left. The herb identifcation garden marked-out with care and order.

Bottom left. Even the outbuildings are surrounded by a riot of color in season.

Far right. A portion of the herb identification garden.

10

Herbal Salads and Spring Delicacies

CAPRILANDS EDIBLE FLOWER SALAD

sour cream or yogurt
chopped dill
chopped chives
2 cups whole beets, cooked,chilled, and finely diced
2 cups chilled carrots, finely diced
2 onions, finely diced
greens
nasturtiums flower heads
calendulas flower heads
violets flower heads

Make a dressing with the sour cream or yogurt and the dill and chives. Arrange the beets, carrots, and onions in separate and attractive segments on the greens and decorate with edible nasturtiums, calendulas and violets.

ROSE COOKIES

1 cup butter
1/2 cup honey
2 eggs, beaten
1 1/4 cups unbleached flour
1 1/2 cups whole wheat flour
1 teaspoon baking soda
1/2 teaspoon cream of tartar
2 tablespoons rose water or 1 teaspoon rose syrup
2 tablespoons caraway seeds
raisins for garnish

Preheat oven to 375 degrees. Cream together butter and honey. Add eggs and beat well. Sift flours with baking soda and cream of tartar.

Add to creamed mixture. Stir in rose water or rose syrup and caraway seeds. Drop mixture by teaspoonfuls onto greased cookie sheets. Flatten slightly with moistened fingers and put a raisin in the center of each cookie. Baked in a 375 degree oven until lightly browned about 8-10 minutes. Remove from cookie sheets and cool on a wire rack.
Makes about 8 dozen.

JOHN EVELYN'S GRAND SALLET OF DIVERS COMPOUNDS

"Take green purslane and pick it leaf by leaf and wash it and swing it in a napkin. Then being dished in a faire, clean dish and finely piled up in a heap in the midst of it, lay round about the center of the sallet, pickled capers, currants and raisins of the sun, washed and picked, mingled and laid round about it; about them some carved cucumbers in slices or halves, and laid round also. Then garnish the dish brims with borage, or clove gillyflowers, or other ways with cucumber peels, olives, capers, and raisins of the sun, then the best Sallet oyl and wine vinegar".

MARIGOLD SOUP

8 cups chicken stock
1/2 cup brown rice, uncooked
1 cup chopped celery
2 medium onions, chopped
2 medium potatoes, scrubbed and diced
1 tablespoon black peppercorns, crushed
2 cups fresh spinach, chopped
2 cups calendula flowers (pot marigold)
1 cup young calendula leaves (pot marigold)
1 tablespoon lemon juice (or more, to taste)
calendula flowers heads for garnish

Far left. A lavish herbal salad, exotic and different, to celebrate the season.

Top left. Delicious rose cookies and a bowl of rose potpourri.

Bottom left. The makings of a salad of herbs sits in the summer's sun immediately after picking.

Combine chicken stock, rice, celery, onions, potatoes and crushed pepper in a large saucepan. Bring to a boil, reduce heat, and simmer, covered for 20 minutes, or until rice is just cooked. Add spinach, chives, parsley, calendula flowers and leaves and cook 5 minutes more. Remove from heat and stir in lemon juice. Garnish with fresh calendula heads. Serve at once with a flower in each bowl.

Serves 10 to 12

SUMMER

Summer Diary

Summer in the herb garden is a time of rare delight when days are long and the plans of winter and the labors of spring come to fruition.

The good care you give your herb garden in summer is the key to its prosperity in all seasons. Summer is the time to accomplish the chores necessary to keep an herb garden healthy for a good harvest.

Summer is the time to water, mulch and feed you garden and make efforts to keep it free of weeds, insects and disease. Finally, we must sow the seed for early fall crops, begin to harvest and preserve our bounty, and take time to gaze upon the garden, now in its full glory, with pleasure and appreciation

Mulching and Feeding

Mulching

After your planting is done, weed the garden clean. Then mulch every bit of bare ground to a depth of 2 inches with buckwheat or cocoa hulls, or other mulching material available in your area. Mix a little sand or soil with these light mulches or wet them down thoroughly for they have a tendency to blow away. As holes appear in the mulch, replenish it. Of all the mulches available today, our choice is cocoa hulls.

A mulch serves several good purposes. It conserves moisture, helps keep down new weeds and gives the garden a neat, well-cared-for appearance.

16

A brick path defines and intrigues in this herb garden.

Feeding

It is true that over-fertilized herbs are not as good for seasonings, on the other hand, an impoverished soil produces stunted plants and poor leaves for cuttings. I find it best to enrich the herb garden scantily with well-rotted manure or "tea" made of rich compost.

Harvesting and Preserving

Drying

As the garden matures, we must start to preserve our harvest so that we may enjoy its fruits through the winter, when fresh leaves are blanketed in snow, slumbering out of reach until the coming spring.

Drying home-grown herbs is one of the great pleasures of herb gardening. It is rewarding to use your own fresh seasonings, and if you dry them, you will doubly appreciate each savory leaf. Drying processes are simple, and the work need not be done all at once for plants mature at different times.

The best time to cut plants for seasoning is before noon after the dew has dried but before the sun has leached the essential oils that keep herbs fresh and flavorful. Of course, herbs should be dried out of direct sun.

Dry herbs in the shade, but not in a damp place. For best color, quick drying is advisable, but heat should not exceed 150 degrees. One method is to spread leaves thinly on a tray of fine wire mesh. This tray is placed in a slow oven with the door left open. Watch carefully as drying should be completed within a matter of minutes, depending on the thickness of the leaves.

Herbs are decoratively hung in bunches from ceiling rafters to dry, or strung on a pole across the front of a fireplace, the original way of curing them. You can still dry herbs by these old-fashioned methods, as long as you do not leave them hanging so long that they pick up dust.

A few herbs need no washing before drying, especially if the garden rows where they grow are mulched thickly with salt hay. However, I wash all leaves excepting those of herbs gathered for seeds, and an occasional tall mint. Washing needs to be done quickly, as warm water releases oils and flavor may be lost if the leaves stay wet for very long.

Herbs to dry in trays include chervil, lovage, myrrh, lemon verbena, parsley, thyme and rosemary. Herbs that dry well hanging in bunches include sage, savory, mint, oregano, marjoram, basil, lemon balm, and horehound. If the bunches are too large, leaves blacken quickly; the flavor will be there if they do not mold, but the color will be unattractive.

Herb seeds to dry include coriander, cumin, caraway, dill, and fennel. Watch these carefully or seeds will fall and be lost. Cut the whole plant, and place it, seed head down, in a paper bag so as to catch all the seeds. Hang up until dry and the seeds will drop out readily. As these seed herbs mature at different times, caraway not until the second year, you will have to be vigilant to save your harvest.

Freezing

Freezing is a simple and effective process for such herbs as sorrel, basil, parsley, dill, chives and chervil. Wash these lightly, then place on paper towels to drain and dry thoroughly. Lie them flat and do not overcrowd them as you freeze. Dried herbs, such as basil, have a distinctly different flavor; frozen basil has a more natural fresh garden taste.

Freezing herbs in ice cubes is recommended if you will be using them in small quantities. The cube when removed from the freezer will melt, leaving the herb ready to use. This method we have found very attractive for herbs for punch, small springs of mint for summer drinks, and sweet woodruff for May wine. You can also freeze borage flowers, violas and tiny marigolds, which are more decorative than flavorful, with the ice cube method.

21

Far left. Fresh herbs start their drying process on wood and mesh racks.

Top left. Herb flavored oils make wonderful additions to salads.

Bottom left. Herbal vinegars add spice and intrigue to salads and cooking.

Herbal Oils and Vinegars

Place harvested leaves from basil, tarragon, thyme or dill in a bottle of white distilled vinegar and steep in the sun. After a week, the vinegar is ready to be stored in a cool cellar where it sets until it is time to place it in smaller, individual bottles. It then comes to the kitchen where it is strained to remove old leaves and any sediment. We pour it through a funnel into smaller containers that may come directly to the table. We place a piece of fresh herb in each bottle to add a decorative and extra added freshness to the final bottling. Spices such as garlic, allspice peppercorns or stick cinnamon can also be added to these vinegars both for taste and appearance.

Preserving herbs in cooking oils provides cooks with excellent assistance in food preparation. A bland, flavorless oil is a good medium for herbal flavorings and is particularly recommended for those who are on a salt free diet. When the herbs are fresh, it takes about two weeks for them to permeate the oil with their essence; if they are dry, allow a longer time, another two weeks. This process may be hastened by heating the oil to the boiling point before pouring it over the herbs. It will then be a good marinade for meat, for some salads, or for frying.

Midsummer Meals

SUMMER SQUASH SOUP

3 medium summer squash (yellow squash preferably)
4 cups chicken stock
1 cup chopped celery
3 medium onions, thinly sliced (about 2 1/2 cups)
1 clove garlic, crushed
1 sprig fresh rosemary, minced
1 sprig fresh thyme, minced
1/2 cup chopped parsley (loosely packed)

Wash, trim, and slice squash, Steam the squash until it is tender. Puree the cooked squash in a blender or food processor and set it aside, (about 1 1/2 cups puree). Bring the chicken stock to a boil in a large saucepan. Add celery, onions, garlic, rosemary and thyme and simmer, covered, about 10 minutes or until vegetables are tender. Reduce heat to low, add reserved squash puree and parsley. Cook to heat through. Yields 7 cups.

MIDSUMMER SALAD

large basil leaves
ripe tomatoes, sliced
red Italian onions, sliced
green onions, chopped
chives, chopped

1 cup honey
parsley, rosemary, chives, thyme, basil
4 cloves garlic, crushed
1/2 cup basil vinegar
sprigs of basil and green onions for garnish

Cover a large platter with basil leaves. Arrange slices of tomatoes and onions so that they overlap. Spread the chopped onions and chives on the top.

Add the herbs to the honey until thick. Mix with vinegar to make a dressing to pour over. Garnish with sprigs of basil and green onions. Hint: This salad is best when the tomatoes are really ripe and basil leaves are crisp and prolific-late July and August at Caprilands.

Right. A festive June punch to herald the coming of summer.

Below. A hollowed-out squash serves as container for the soup made from its flesh.

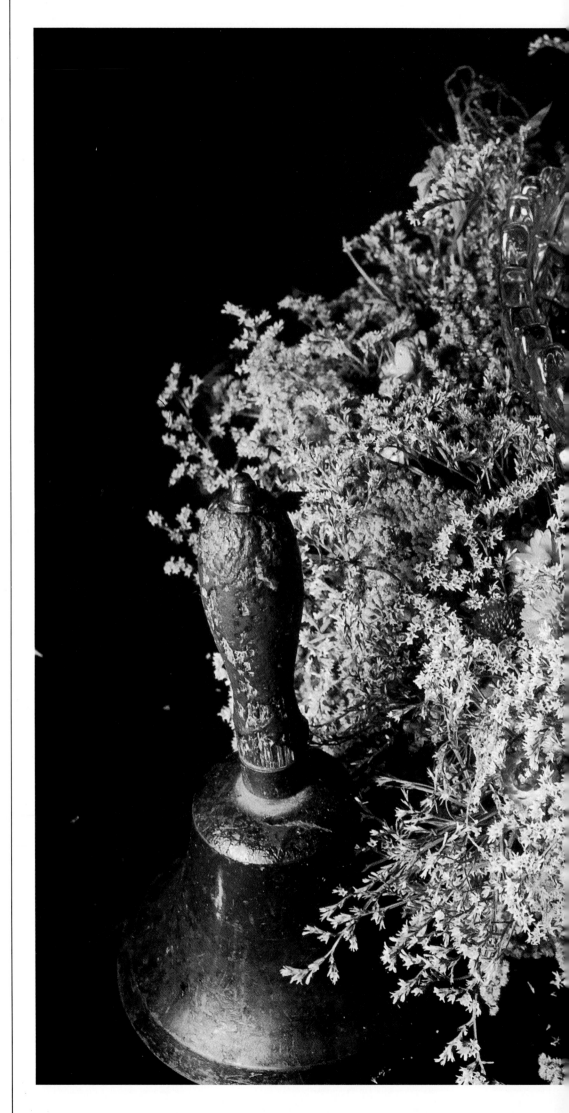

JUNE PUNCH

1 cup rosemary leaves
3 stalks borage, stem, leaves and blossoms
1 gallon grape or apple juice or mixture
3 limes, juice of
1/2 cup honey
1/2 cup brown sugar
1 lime, sliced for garnish
borage leaves and blossoms for garnish

Steep rosemary and borage in juices, honey and sugar in large jug, three hours at room temperature, or preferably 24 hours or longer in the refrigerator. At serving time, pour juice mixture over block of ice in punch bowl. Decorate with lime slices, fresh blossoms, and leaves. Hint: In late summer, we heap the cake of ice with peace slices and ladle a slice into each cup. Makes 1 gallon.

CARROT AND ORANGE SOUP

2 tablespoons butter
2 medium onions, chopped
8 large carrots, scrubbed and sliced (about 5 cups)
3 cups chicken broth
1/4 teaspoon white pepper
1/4 teaspoon ground cloves
2 tablespoons flour
1 clove garlic, chopped
1 teaspoon chopped shallots
1/2 cup fresh mint leaves, loosely packed
juice of 1/2 lemon
2 cups orange juice

Melt butter in a large saucepan. Add onions and saute over medium heat until soft. Add carrots, chicken broth, pepper and ground cloves.

Cover and simmer over medium heat until carrots are tender, about 15 minutes. Remove about 1/4 cup of stock. Mix flour with stock and return it to the pan. Cook, stirring, about 5 minutes longer. Remove pan from heat and cool 15-20 minutes. Stir garlic, shallots and mint into cooled soup.

Puree the soup in batches in a food processor or blender until smooth. Pour pureed soup into a serving bowl, stir in lemon and orange juices, cover and chill thoroughly. Serve soup in chilled bowls, garnished with orange slices or mint. Serves 12 (8 cups).

29

The wonderful abundance of herbs and flowers fills one of the rooms at Caprilands.

32

Top right. Delicately scented rose potpourri makes a splendid gift and scents the house with its dusky aroma.

Bottom right. A mixed potpourri can be varied according to what's available and the seasons.

Far right. Lemon verbena, with its sweet and spicy lemon scent, refreshes the senses wherever it's used.

Fixatives from the animal world are also used to hold the fragrance of potpourri ingredients. Animal fixatives include ambergris, civet and musk. Often the odor of the fixative is disagreeable, but when combined with fragrant things, it absorbs and enhances the essences.

When essences or essential oils are included in recipes, the distilled plant oil is indicated. These are generally volatile oils that evaporate at room temperature. They occur in secretory cells, reservoirs, glands of flowers, barks, fruits, and leaves. Most oils are obtained by steam distillation.

Attar of roses is the most fabulous and desirable of all oils. It is said that it takes ten thousand pounds of rose petals to make one pound of oil. Other oils used in the making of potpourri include oil of violet, carnation, jasmine, lemon verbena, and orange blossom.

Priceless Potpourri

LEMON VERBENA JAR

1 cup dried lemon verbena leaves
1 cup dried lemon balm leaves
rind of 1 lemon, dried and grated
1/2 cup each dried petals from forsythia, calendula, lemon-
scented dwarf marigold
1 ounce orris root with 6 drops of lemon verbena oil
leaves of lemon-scented thyme, optional

Combine all ingredients, then turn into small apothecary jars. Press some of the yellow flowers against the sides of the jar for color. Tie the top with yellow and green velvet ribbon.

ROSE JAR

1 quart dried rose petals
1 cup each dried lavender flowers and rose geranium leaves
1/2 cup patchouli
1/2 cup sandalwood chips and vetiver, mixed
2 teaspoons of frankincense and myrrh, mixed
1 teaspoon each of powdered benzoin, cinnamon and cloves
2 tonka beans, ground
1/4 cup allspice
10 drops rose oil
1 cup orris root

Mix first eight ingredients thoroughly; then add the rose oil and orris root. Mix again and stir well. If this amount of orris seems excessive, remember that this is a basic mixture to which you can add flowers of the season right up to fall. After it is finished, close the jar for at least two weeks (a month is better), then it will be ready to enjoy.

MINT POTPOURRI

2 cups dried lavender
1 cup dried mint leaves (peppermint, spearmint or orange
mint)
1/2 cup dried culinary thyme
1/4 cup rosemary
few drops of essential oils of lavender, thyme and bergamot
dried red geranium petals, blue bachelor's-button, and
delphinium

Combine ingredients and store in apothecary jars. When you're entertaining, turn some of this mixture out into a pewter or silver bowl. Stir slightly and the smell of a fresh clean breeze will permeate the room. An excellent potpourri for a desk or worktable, perhaps in a widemouth, antique sugarbowl of stoneware or old blue Staffordshire.

37

The house at Caprilands decorated for the Christmas holidays.

MOIST POTPOURRI

3 cups dried rose petals
1 cup bay salt
1 teaspoon each of allspice, cinnamon, and coriander
1 tablespoon each of cloves, grated nutmeg and anise
1 cup dried lavender
1/4 cup of patchouli leaves and powdered orris root
1/4 ounce each of oil of rose and oil of rose geranium
3 cups of a mixture made of dried rosemary, lemon balm
and lemon verbena leaves.

In a covered crock, mix rose petals with the bay salt and leave for one week, turning daily. Add spices and let stand for another week, turning daily. At the end of two weeks add the lavender, patchouli, orris root, and oils. Let stand for a few weeks, then mix in leaves of dried rosemary, lemon balm, and lemon verbena. Stir frequently with a wooden spoon or cinnamon stick.

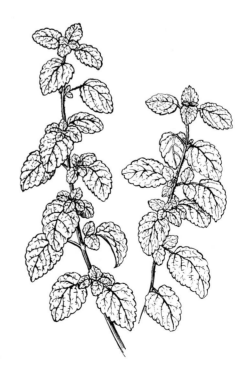

WINTER

Winter Diary

The quiet aloneness of winter has a special charm for the herb gardener, and I confess this season is my delight. Through the restless, rushing hours of spring, and the long days of summer that begin at dawn and end with weeding in the twilight, I find myself looking back at the peace of the past winter, and forward to the next one. The winter landscape, bare and stringent, reveals a beauty of form and line that is not visible in spring and summer.

Through the small-paned windows of my northwest writing room, the winter landscape stretches toward the surrounding woodland providing a perfect setting to dream and plan next year's garden, and plans for the coming holiday season.

Christmas is the peak of the herb gardener's year, a time of long preparation, great anticipation and much excitement. The herb gardener has a wealth of materials to put to use in holiday celebrations This is the time to make use of your herb garden; to make personal gifts that money cannot buy; to construct beautiful flower and herb wreaths to celebrate the season, and to fill the house with color and the sweet odor of evergreen and rosemary.

A Time to Plan

Winter is the time to enjoy the planning of an herb garden, and these plans become increasingly ambitious with the reading of books, magazines, and catalogs. Even though the plan must be revised to make it practical when unseen obstacles become sudden realities in spring, still basic winter planning is necessary and worthwhile.

Whether the herb garden is small or large, it needs to be exquisitely neat and weedless, with wide paths and compact borders, the same plant often repeated to make a good showing. A background is impor-

Top right. An Advent wreath en-
lived with glowing tapers.

Bottom right. Drying herbs and
flowers brighten the cold days of
winter.

Far right. Forms and wreath
bases, along with flowers, reeds
and herbs are the beginnings of
wreath-making.

42

tant, a hedge, wooden fence, or stone wall, perhaps with espaliered trees. For new gardens by modern houses a fence of cedar, redwood, or grape stake looks well. This encloses the garden, and furnishes support for taller plants and vines. Your herb garden is not complete unti there is a place for yu to sit comfortably with room for a companion or two.

A good plan is all important for a garden that is full of delights. Certainly the most difficult garden is the one that is unplanned. The most delightful way to spend the the long weeks of winter is in contemplation and planning of the next season's herb garden.

Wreaths from the Herb Garden

The making of wreaths is an ancient and honored art that began about a thousand years before the birth of Christ. A crown of oak leaves adorned the warrior, ivy rewarded the poet, and statesmen were dignified under their laurels. Roman generals were crowned as they returned from war with wreaths made of grass and wild flowers from the battlefields.

At Christmas, the wreath is symbolic of Christian immortality. The circle and the sphere are symbols of eternal life. Traditionally, the wreath has been worn at festivals, at sacrifices, at weddings, and banquets. Brides wore coronets of orange blossoms, myrtle or rosemary. Funeral wreaths were made of daffodils, poppies, and other plants that meant remembrance. At Caprilands, we mark special holidays with beautiful wreaths, constructed out of herbs symbolic of the occasion.

Herb Bases

During the growing season, we make living wreaths out of the fresh flowers and herbs flourishing in the garden, and later out of evergreens kept fresh throughout the holiday season. In winter we construct everlasting wreaths out of dried garden material arranged on a base of silver king artemisia.

To make a living wreath base, you will need a hollow circle planting-form about 12 inches across. Fill it with moist, unmilled sphagnum moss. Place this on a black or dark green metal tray, or on an old pewter plate, to make watering possible. Insert cuttings of green santolina thickly all the way around the circle so as to cover the brown moss. All this forms the base of the wreath and stays fresh and green indefinitely if it is kept moist and out of the sun.

To make an everlasting base of artemisia, you will need a circular wire wreath frame. Arrange artemisia stalks thickly and evenly arund the wire. Let stems overlap and press them down and bind lightly with florist's wire. Flatten the artemisia, adding more wire where necessary. This forms the base on which to place your best cuttings.

The Living Wreath

On a sphagnum moss base, arrange green Santolina cuttings along the outer edge. Then group lavender and a rosette of lamb's-ears on one side, spreading out the leaves to make a flower like shape. On the opposite side, insert a rosette of young horehound plants. Sage, gold thyme and rue make fine accents.

Advent Wreath

Another wreath made on a sphagnum moss base is the Advent wreath, made of herbs associated with Christmas. I use Savin, juniper, rosemary, Our Lady's bedstraw, thyme, pennyroyal, rue, lavender, horehound, sage, true myrtle and the purple, white, and pink flowers of dried globe amaranth. Mechanics are the same as for the living wreath.

Cover the moist sphagnum moss with clippings of Savin juniper inserted thickly and deeply right into the wire frame. Press four pieces of floral clay, each large enough to hold the base of a 12-inch candle, and place these clay holders equidistant around the wreath. Complete the wreath with other herbal materials and small bows of purple velvet, changing these to pink for the third Sunday.

Top far left. One of the Capri-lands' staff demonstrates the joys of wreath-making.

Bottom far left. A herb and spice wreath will make anyone feel warmer on a cold winter's day.

Left. The best china and fragrant, freshly-brewed tea are the perfect antidote for winter's chill.

An Everlasting Wreath of Artemisia

Take your whitest artemisia (if you want a brown effect, use plants harvested later), remove the curls or stems from the tree-like blossoms, or cut the tops from the wispy ones that have not properly developed, and cut with stems long enough to insert in the base. Turn the curls toward the center, working clockwise until the circle is filled. Shape the outside line carefully as you work to keep a good circle.

The wreath is now ready for floral decoration. Add a circle of tansy, then use yarrow toward the bottom. Make a circle of the everlastings, pressing their soft stems among the sturdier ones already in the wreath. Follow these with a ring of oregano, then ambrosia on the inside of the circle or pushed into the design for a green, mossy effect. Use the St. John's-wort and rue pods as pins and add small sprigs of dried lance-leaf goldenrod to give the design liveliness. Bows of yellow and brown velvet with a group of small cones or a rosette of tiny brass bells complete the festive appearance of this everlasting wreath.

An Herb and Spice Wreath

This fragrant and attractive circle of spices and herbs makes a perfect decoration for the kitchen. Use the artemisia base, adding a circle of bay leaves with the lower edge left open. Point the bay leaves toward the center of the circle. In the lower edge arrange one of two nutmegs. Group three cinnamon sticks and wire them into the nutmeg, then ad cardamom in the same cluster. The finishing touch consists of sprigs or rosemary inserted all around the outside of the wreath for a green frame.

Winter Tea Party

In midwinter with the garden at rest and the holidays behind me, I turn my energy to the greenhouse and writing table, with time left each day to sip a cup of fragrant tea. Tea-drinking was the favorite social pastime of the American colonists. With the tax on tea representing injustice, patriotic ladies banished real tea from their tables and turned to other leaves for a satisfying beverage.

Camomile Tea

The mature flowers of two plants, Chrysanthemum parthenium and Anthemis nobilis, are harvested for this. The petals disappear when dry and only the yellow seed heads remain. They yield a slightly bitter brew that is refreshing for headaches and nausea, good for the nerves, and is soporific. This is a household medicine and one of the most popular drinks in Europe. Allow a heaping teaspoonful of the seed heads to a cup of water; brew in a teapot. Strain before serving and sweeten with honey if desired.

Caprilands Tea

Remembering the many virtues that herbs have and could contribute to our well being, I have mixed a tea or rich symbolism. If you drink it, theoretically you should enjoy these benefits: wisdom from mint, memory from rosemary, immortality and domestic happiness from sage, bravery from thyme, happiness from marjoram, a good complexion and a bright outlook on life from calendula, and soothed nerves and a good night's sleep from camomile. Furthermore, this tea tastes good. To make it, mix equal parts of the dried herbs and allow 1 heaping teaspoonful to 1 cup of boiling water.

Mint Tea

Mint is the herb most associated with teas. Mentha piperita is the strongest of the flowers and in its own right without other herbs, makes a good drink for those who wish to replace China tea or coffee as a beverage. Peppermint was used medicinally for heat prostration and to avert or cure nausea. We cut mint (particularly apple mint) about three times in the season for a magnificent harvest. We store the leaves in airtight cans and in winter use them in a mixed herb tea with this mint for a base.

48

Harvesting scented geraniums at
Caprilands.

Catnip

Nepeta cataria

Hardy perennial, 2 to 3 feet. Sturdy stems, straight and similar to other mints, square and set with leaves 2 to 3 inches long, downy, heart-shaped, green above, gray below. Flowers are pale purplish in dense clusters on spikes. Propagate by division of roots in spring in sun or partial shade in sandy or rich soil. Catnip self-sows once established. Cats usually like the dried leaves and blossoms better than fresh. A tea brewed from dried leaves may be used to soothe the nerves.

Chervil

Anthriscus cerefolium

Annual, 1 to 2 feet. Leaves alternate, fern-like, and spreading. The plant resembles Italian parsley, though more delicate, and turns reddish in the Fall. Small white flowers in compound umbels. Sow seeds in early spring in moist, well-drained soil. Sow again in late summer for a fall harvest. Self-sows year after year. Attractive in garden. Use leaves in salads, soups, with oysters, and as a garnish.

Chives

Allium schoenoprasum

Hardy perennial to 1 foot, producing fountains of hollow, cylindrical leaves. Sow seeds in spring or fall in sunny, well-drained garden loam. Takes nearly a year to establish from seed. Divide established clumps every three or four years. Plant as borders. Cut the leaves for soups and salads from early spring on. Use in cream cheese mixtures, with mashed potatoes, in hamburger, or with eggs in omelettes. Chives can be frozen or dried for winter seasoning.

Coriander

Coriandrum sativum

Annual, 2 feet. Leaves finely cut like parsley. Delicate flowers in umbels, rosy lavender, appearing in late June. Sow seeds in spring in full sun and well-drained, moist, and fertile soil. Harvest seeds as early as possible or they will bend the weak stems to the ground and be lost. Use in curry, chopped meat, stews, sausage, gingerbread, cookies and candies.

Costmary

Chrysanthemum balsamita

Hardy perennial, 2 to 3 feet, stiff stems with erect branches, short, and slightly downy. Leaves 6 to 8 inches long with toothed margins. Flowers small, button-like, pale yellow, resembling tansy. Thrives in well-drained soil and full sun, but will grow in semishade. Propagate by root division in spring or fall. Divide plants every third year. Use fresh or dried for tea and iced drinks. Place in closets and drawers, along with lavender, for a sweet odor.

Dill

Anethum graveolens

Hardy annual sometimes classified as a biennial, 2 to 2 1/2 feet. The plant is upright, branching out from a single stalk with the feathery leaves which are known to cooks as dill weed. Numerous yellow flowers in flat terminal umbels, followed by dill seed in mid-summer. Plant in rich, sandy, well-drained soil in full sun in spring. Harvest dill weed leaves in early summer, then chop fine and dry n a basket, turning often. Harvest the seeds as soon as the head is ripe. Plant with coriander, caraway, and anise. Use dill to flavor pickles and herb vinegars.

Fennel

Foeniculum vulgare

Perennial sometimes grown as an annual, 4 to 5 feet. The stems are blue-green, smooth and glossy, flattened at base;leaves, bright green and feathery. Yellow flowers are produced in umbels. Sow seeds in the early spring in full sun and average garden soil. Use tender leaves and stems in relishes, salads, and as a garnish. Use leaves for flavoring in fish sauces, soups, and stews, ripe seeds to flavor puddings, spiced beers, sauerkraut, spaghetti, soups, breads, cakes, candy and beverages.

Feverfew

Chrysanthemum parthenium

Hardy perennial, 2 to 3 feet. Leaves light green with strong daisy-like odor. Sow sets or set out plants in early spring. Prefer sun to partial shade in moist, well-drained soil. Divide established plants every fall or spring, replanting only the strongest divisions. Use in perennial flower borders and as a cut flower.

Germander

Teucrium lucidum

Hardy perennial, 1 to 1 1/2 feet. This plant lends itself to clipping as a small hedge and resembles boxwood. The leaves are small, stiff, and glossy dark green, the edges toothed. Flowers are magenta, but best kept cut off so that the plants will stay bushy and full as a hedge. Propagate by rooting cuttings early in the growing season in full sun and well-drained, moist garden loam. Cover with salt hay in the winter time. Use as a small hedge for the perennial border or herb garden.

Heliotrope

Valeriana officinalis

Hardy perennial, 3 to 5 feet. Leaves lance-shaped in pairs. Flowers pale pink in flattened cluster starting in June. Propagate by removing side-shoots of old plants. Set firmly and deeply so that animals will not catch the odor and dig up the root. Thrives in sun or shade in rich, moist, garden soil. Use as an attractive flowering herb for the back of the border.

Horehound

Marrubium vulgare

Perennial, only half-hardy in severely cold climates, grows to 2 feet. Leaves are wrinkled and almost white, forming rosettes in early growth. Full sun and sandy, dry soil. Except in mild climates, treat as a biennial, sowing a few seeds each year. Horehound can also be propagated by making cuttings in the spring or summer, or by division in spring. Use as flavoring for famous horehound candy; as a tea to treat

coughs and as a syrup for children's coughs and colds.

Hyssop
Hyssopus officinalis

Hardy perennial, 1 to 1 1/2 feet. Leaves are narrow, small and pointed, dark green on woody stems. Flowers dark blue, pink or white in spikes. Bears slight resemblance to boxwood. Sow seeds in well-prepared, moist soil in spring. Prefers full sun and alkaline soil. Plant near grapes, use as a tea for plant bacteria. Plant as a hedge, and use blossoms for cutting.

Lamb's-Ear
Stachys olympica

Hardy perennial, 1 to 3 feet. Leaves are long-stemmed and linear, heavily covered by white hairs that give the plant a beautiful silvery appearance and softness to the touch. Flowers purple, in spikes. Propagate by division in spring or fall and plant in full sun in moist, well-drained soil. Use for flower arrangements and as showy border plants.

Lavender
Lavandula officinalis

Hardy perennial, 1 to 3 feet. A woody semishrub that is many branched with narrow leaves, 1 to 2 inches long, gray-green and velvety. Flowers small and lavender. Difficult to grow from seed. Propagate from slips with the heel attached in moist sand in late July. Divide plants after blooming. Plant in sunny, well-drained, alkaline soil. Do not trim in the early spring; wait to trim until blooms have been harvested. Bug free. A moth preventative.Use dried leaves and flowers in potpourri. Oil of lavender is used in soaps and perfumes.

Lavender-Cotton
Santolina chamaecyparissus

Hardy perennial, 1 to 2 feet. Leaves very fine, yet sturdy; gray to white at certain seasons, but blue-gray while young. The few flowers are globular and yellow. Propagate by rooting cuttings in sand or vermi-

Angelica.

Anise.

Basil.

Camomile.

Chive blossoms.

Dill.

Juniper.

Lavender.

Lemon Balm.

Oregano.

Parsley.

Rosemary.

Sorrel.

Spearmint

Tarragon.

Borage.

Burnet.

Bronze Fennel.

Fennel.

Lemon Verbena.

Orange Mint.

Rue.

Sage.

Thyme.

culite. Transport rooted cuttings into small pots until they make balls of roots, then move in full sun in average garden soil, either dry or moist but perfectly drained. Trim carefully in the fall as santolinas do not die back to the ground but come out along the old wood.

Lemon Balm

Melissa officinalis

Hardy perennial, 1 to 2 feet, with branches growing n a square stem. Leaves broadly heart-shaped, toothed, 1 to 3 inches long. Sow seeds in any soil, but best in a well-drained location. Needs sun half a day, but will grow in shade. Bug free. Makes an excellent mild tea. Good also for punch, for claret cup, fruit desserts, and as a garnish for fish. The dry leaves are used in potpourri.

Lemon Verbena

Lippia citriodora

Tender perennial, to 6 feet as a tubbed plant. Leaves yellow-green indoors, glossy and darker outdoors. Lemon verbena can be trained as a topiary tree but is very sensitive to change. There is no readily available or viable seed; plants are grown from cuttings and are not easily propagated. Dry the leaves for potpourri and to steep for tea. Fresh leaves may be used to garnish salads or to make jellies and desserts.

Lovage

Levisticum officinale

Hardy perennial, 3 to 5 feet. A vigorous, coarse plant. Leaves dark green resembling celery in appearance, odor, and taste. Flowers small, greenish, in small umbels, not decorative. May be propagated by division in spring or from seeds in autumn. Cover them lightly and germination should occur the following spring. Prefers partial shade in fertile, deep, and evenly moist soil.Bug repellent. Harvest tender leaves for soups, stews, potato salad, salad greens, sauces. Blanch stems and eat as celery. The seeds, shole or ground, make cordials and may be used in meat pies, salads, and candies.

Oregano
Origanum vulgare

Hardy perennial, 2 feet. Leaves dull, gray-green, oval, with stems often purple. Flowers pink, white, purple or lilac. Propagate by division of established plants in the spring, by rooting cuttings, or by sowing seeds. Prefers full sun and average garden soil, on the dry side but well-drained. Use leaves, fresh or dried, in spaghetti sauce, sparingly in salads, on tomatoes, and in herb seasoning mixtures.

Our Lady's Bedstraw
Galium verum

Hardy perennial, 2 feet. Dainty foliage creeps along the ground in spring, but grows taller in July, when the stems become stiff and dry. Obtain plants and, after they become established and have multiplied, divide the roots in spring using the young offshoots. Prefers full sun to partial shade in average garden soil, even in unmanageable problem areas provided they are well-drained. Use as a filler in flower arrangements and as a dye plant. Useful as a spreading plant that can crowd out weeds in problem areas.

Parsley
Petroselinum crispum

Hardy biennial usually cultivated as an annual. It has bright green, tightly curled leaves and makes an excellent border for the culinary garden. Italian parsley, also a hardy biennial cultivated as an annual, has large plain leaves reminiscent of a fern which may be cut in quantity for salad greens, or cooked as a vegetable. Grow from seed from earliest spring through midsummer in full sun or partial shade in humusy, moist soil. Grow with tomatoes. Cut all through the season, using generously in salads, soups, casseroles, and omelettes with other vegetables.

Rosemary

Rosmarinum officinalis

Tender perennial, 3 to 6 feet. Needle-like leaves vary in color from gray-green to dark green, depending upon variety. The blossoms may be white-rose, pale lavender, pale or dark blue. Root cuttings in sand or vermiculite using 4 to 6 inch pieces of new wood or healthy ends tips. Seeds are not difficult to germinate, but are usually slow to grow and require three years to bloom. Prefers full sun to partial shade with evenly moist, well-drained, and alkaline soil. Plant with sage. Wards off the cabbage worm and bean beetle. Use green or dried, sparingly on chicken, in gravy with lamb, in soup, stuffings, sauces, dressings, in jelly, and as a tea.

Rue

Ruta graveolens

Hardy perennial, 3 feet. Leaves alternate, blue-green, musky smelling, much divided and noticed on erect, stout woody stems. Yellow flowers resembling a cluster of stars are followed by red-brown seed pods that look hand carved. Propagate by dividing old plants in late spring or, after blooming, by rooting cuttings or sowing seeds in full sun and average garden soil, preferably dry, stony and alkaline. Use as an ornamental plant toward the back of the border where it will have little opportunity to cause skin irritations, for which it is known. Repels horseflies and house flies, aphids, blackfly. The dried seed heads are excellent for use in wreaths and swags.

Sage

Salvia officinalis

Hardy perennial, 3 feet. Leaves oblong, gray and pebbly, on stiff stems that become woody and gnarled with age. Flowers blue in whorls. Seeds of common sage sown in early spring in a sunny site with moist, well-drained garden soil will produce fine plants for cutting by fall. Plant with rosemary, for carrots, peas, broccoli, Brussels spouts. Cut leaves of common sage at any time for cheese sandwiches, souffles, and stuffings. Use dried in sausages, with cheese, pork, poultry, to season stuffing in turkey, and as a tea.

Salad Burnet

Sanguisorba minor

Hardy perennial, 1 to 2 feet, evergreen. Leaves bear a similarity to those of the wild rose and remain nearly flat on the ground until flowering time. Flowers deep but pale crimson in a round head. Sow seeds in late fall, early spring, and summer in sun and well-drained, alkaline soil. Use fresh leaves that smell of cucumber for salads, vinegars, cream cheese, drinks, seasoning green butters, and as a garnish. This is one of the most decorative of herbs, worthy of space in most gardens.

Sorrel

Rumex scutatus

Hardy perennial, 2 feet. Resembles the related and common dock of the fields. Leaves succulent, long and shield-shaped, light green in color. Flowers a warm red-brown color. Buy a plant, then allow to multiply in sun to partial shade in rich, well-drained soil. Use in sorrel soup, sparingly in salads, as a sauce for beef, or cooked with beet tops, spinach or cabbage. Cut early in the spring and freeze some leaves for use later in the year.

Summer Savory

Satureja hortensis

Annual, 1 to 1 1/2 feet. Leaves narrow, dark green, on stout stems that become branched and tree-like in late summer. Flowers pale lavender or pure white. Sow seeds in early spring. Broadcast in a wide, well-prepared row. Mulch with salt hay to prevent weeds and to keep leaves clean for cutting. Prefers a sunny location in well-drained garden loam. Cut two or three times during the drying season, preferably before the blossoms form. Plant with beans, repels the bean beetle. Use in cooking green beans, for all bean dishes in stuffings, with rice, in soups, gravies, and sauces.

Sweet Basil
Ocimum basilicum

Annual, to 2 feet. Leaves 1 to 2 inches long, shining dark green and pointed. The flowers are white or purplish in spikes. Sow seeds after the weather has warmed in the spring. Friendly to all in the garden. Plant with tomatoes. Prefers sun to partial shade in average, but moist garden soil. Use leaves in salads, vinegars, spaghetti, soups, with meat, game, fish, and tomato dishes. Excellent also in flower arrangements.

Sweet Cicely
Myrrhis odorata

Hardy perennial, 2 to 3 feet. The long thick root sends up branching stems of fragrant, anise-scented leaves. The white flowers appear in late May and early June and are followed by seeds an inch long and dark brown when ripe. To grow seeds, plant in autumn while the seeds are still fresh. Transplant to permanent positions in the spring, allowing plenty of space for mature plants. Prefers shady, moist soil. Use the spicy seeds fresh and green in herb mixtures as a spice. Use the leaves in salads or as a filling in pastries. Roots may be eaten like fennel, raw or boiled.

Sweet Marjoram
Origanum majorana

Tender perennial, grown as an annual in the North, to 1 foot. Leaves gray-green, rounded and velvety. Flowers in white clusters have knot-like shapes before blossoming. Sow seeds in carefully pulverized soil in spring. Cover lightly with shredded sphagnum moss and keep moist. Prefers full sun in well-drained alkaline soil. Plants are attractive in a border. Use fresh or dried leaves in soups, in stuffings for pork or lamb, and with eggs. The leaves may also be used in potpourri and steeped for tea.

Tansy

Tanacetum vulgare

Hardy perennial, 3 feet. Attractive plant with coarse fern-like leaves. Flowers like yellow buttons in clusters. Tansy is best when planted against a fence that will give it some protection from high winds and rains. Propagate by division in sun to partial shade in almost any soil provided it is not wet for long periods. Controls ants, aphids, flies, fleas, moths, Japanese beetles. Good for compost; use leaves for moth preventative. Dry the flowers as everlastings for fall and winter arrangements, wreaths, and swags.

Violet

Viola odorata

The sweet English violet is partial to full shade in humus, moist soil. Propagate by dividing well established clumps after they finish blooming. Violets can become troublesome weeds, so guard them closely. Attractive border and ground cover. Candy the flowers for use on tops of cakes. Use them fresh in punch, in flower arrangements, and in miniature winter plantings where they will provide bloom out of season. Violets are used in May wine along with strawberries, and there is a violet jelly, violet sherbet, and even violet fritters.

Yarrow

Achillea millefolium

Hardy perennial, to 2 feet. Leaves gray-green, finely divided, giving name milfoil (thousand leaves). Flowers grayish white or pale lavender in flattened clusters. Propagate by dividing roots, spring or fall; or transplant self sown seedlings. Increases the aromatic quality of all herbs, helps vegetables. Use in flower arrangements, fresh or dried. Ironclad garden perennials for late spring and summer color.